MW01279942

POSSESSING
THE KINGDOM

*Rediscovering
Kingdom Identity*

JESSE SACKEY

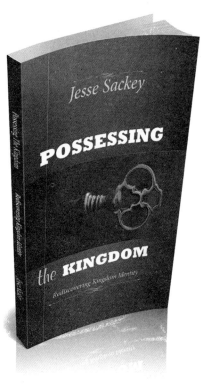

Jesse Sackey

POSSESSING

the KINGDOM

Rediscovering Kingdom Identity

POSSESSING THE KINGDOM
Rediscovering Kingdom Identity

All Bible references are taken from the New King James Version, unless otherwise stated.

Author's Contact: *revjesses1@gmail.com*

The opinions expressed by the author are not necessarily those of Rehoboth House. Rehoboth House is committed to excellence and best practices in printing and publishing, according to industry standards.

EBook: 978-1-60796-929-7
Paperback: 978-0-9964267-5-6
Hardcover: 978-0-9964267-6-3

Published in the United Sates of America
By Rehoboth House, Chicago.
www.rehobothhouseonline.com

REHOBOTH HOUSE

Table Of Contents

ACKNOWLEDGEMENT

My deepest gratitude goes to my Lord God Almighty for his grace and enablement to write this book. To my dear wife, Harriet and our children Gloria, Joshua, David and Ed, I say thank you for your love, support, encouragement and standing strongly with me through all times. I love you all dearly. I also appreciate my pastors and people of Latter Rain Family Chapel for being there to hear these Kingdom series developed. Let me again say a big thank you to Pastor and Mrs. Emeka Joshua Emeruem of Rehoboth House, Chicago for their hard work in seeing this work published. My deep appreciation also goes to Rev. Dr. Gabriel Amoateng Boahen of Chicago. A dear man of God whom the Lord has blessed with anointed sons, (Prophet Sampson Amoateng, Prophet Dr. Mark Amoateng, Prophet Daniel Amoateng and Prophet Brian Amoateng) who are all doing great ministry to the glory of God. Thank you for your friendship and doing me the honour of writing the foreword of this book. God richly bless you all.

Acknowledgement

DEDICATION

I dedicate this book to Rev. Victor and First Lady Georgina Owusu-Teng of Church Of The Living God, Chicago, USA for being great friends and my hosts together with your family over the years and for encouraging me to produce books. Your home has been more than an abode to me. I have received a lot every time I have been there. You have been a great blessing to me, my family and ministry. Thank you and God bless you all abundantly.

Dedication

INTRODUCTION

One of the greatest tragedies in the Body of Christ today is an identity crisis that has led to non-fulfillment of the counsel and purposes of God in the lives of many believers. Some have lost their Kingdom identity while others have a distorted view of who they are in Christ. Until you rediscover your real Kingdom identity, possessing your possessions remains elusive. This unfortunate situation has led to untold hardships and frustration among God's people.

It is evident that in our society today, if you cannot define your real identity, you lose most of your rights and privileges. This has been the situation with many believers of our time. The prerequisite for you possessing your inheritance in the Kingdom therefore, is to define your identity in the light of the infallible word of God.

Friend, if you are in any of the above situations, I believe God has put this book in your hands to help you rediscover your Kingdom identity and stir you to rise up and possess what has been freely given to you in Christ Jesus. This is because God wants to take you to another level in your walk with Him and to bring you into fulfillment in this life.

FOREWORD

Under the inspiration of the Holy Spirit, the author raises identity crisis as a grave concern in his introductory remarks, and further amplifies the simple reason that some Christians today have sadly lost their identity or have an obscure understanding of who they are in Christ. Consequently, this has led to some painful experiences in their lives and non-accomplishment of God's plan for them.

> *"I know what I'm doing. I have it all planned out — plans to take care of you, not abandon you, plans to give you the future you hope for" (Jeremiah 29:11). THE MESSAGE*

God knows where the Body of Christ stands at such a time like this, especially with the work of the Kingdom He has entrusted to us as believers. He therefore brings in our way a timely and most needed book; *Possessing The Kingdom: Rediscovering Kingdom Identity* by his beloved son, Rev. Jesse Sackey of the Latter Rain Family Chapel, Ghana.

This book was written purposely for our personal renewal (Rom. 12:1-2), revival (Ps. 119:156) and rejuvenation. I therefore encourage you to avail yourself to breathe fresh spiritual air and be repositioned to possess what is yours for the Kingdom. For me, it is a wake-up call to the Body of Christ in this time of reclamation, restoration and re-possession of whatever the enemy stole from us due to spiritual ignorance, lethargy, compromise and friendship with the world (James 4:4). The author, throughout the pages of this book, urges us to arise in power and take back what belongs to us.

The popular saying "knowledge is power" is still relevant today. In normal life, a young, brilliant and knowledgeable lawyer defends his many clients in court and is equally so tough for his colleagues, citing the appropriate, on-target cases or articles in his submission to the amazement of the sitting judge. Similarly, an enterprising business executive maximizes every opportunity to make an astronomical profit. In the same vein, the Christian must study the word of God to have the fullest knowledge about one's identity and position in Christ Jesus without any ambiguity. This is exactly what the author has sought to promote with the many biblical references about the Christian's identity.

Thank you, Rev. Jesse Sackey, for hearing the voice of God correctly and responding accordingly in humility with this Kingdom exhortation.

I am very humbled and honored to write the Foreword for this timely book for our generation, which is fast gaining awareness to pursue Kingdom mindedness to the Glory of God.

Dr. Gabriel Amoateng-Boahen
Professional Staff Chaplain (Retired),
University of Chicago Medical Center,
Chicago, Illinois, USA, & Founder and President,
Royal Diadem Pastoral Center.

CHAPTER 1
Take Your
POSSESSION

"And I bestow upon you a kingdom, just as My Father bestowed one upon Me" (Luke 22:29).

"Rise, take your journey, and cross over the River Arnon. Look, I have given into your hand Sihon the Amorite, king of Heshbon, and his land. Begin to possess it, and engage him in battle" (Deut. 2:24-25).

The Lord has given us a kingdom to possess; the Kingdom of God. However, in this life, anywhere there is a vacuum somebody or something fills it. Even nature abhors vacuum. We need to be informed and become aware of it so we can take possession and fulfill the purpose for which God gave it.

Let us understand that when God told Israel He was giving them the land of Canaan to possess, that territory was already occupied by certain forces, possibly stronger than the Jews. God did not promise them a vacant land. In other words, their divinely given possessions were already in the hands of some others. The implication was that, for them to enter and possess their possession, they had to engage the occupants in battle. So it is today!

> *'"Rise, take your journey, and cross over the River Arnon. Look, I have given into your hand Sihon the Amorite, king of Heshbon, and his land. <u>Begin to possess it, and engage him in battle</u>" (Deut 2:24).*

They are things (both spiritual and physical) God has already allotted to you, even before you were born.

> *"Blessed be the God and Father of our Lord Jesus Christ, who has blessed us with every spiritual blessing in the heavenly places in Christ" (Ephesians 1:3).*

But the same Ephesians 6:12 says;
> *"For we do not wrestle against flesh and blood, but against principalities, against powers, against the rulers of the darkness of this age, against spiritual hosts of wickedness in the heavenly places" (Ephesians 6:12).*

2

In the same heavenly places where our blessings have been determined are also found spiritual wickedness. If you lack this understanding you may not have the drive to engage the adversary in battle in order to reclaim what belongs to you. So don't just get excited when the scripture says you shall possess your possessions. You have to dispossess those holding them in order to possess the things God has already given to you. Settle that once and for all in your mind.

Obadiah1:17-21 says;
"Upon Mt. Zion shall be deliverance and there shall be holiness and the house of Jacob shall possess their possessions".

But listen to this;
"And the house of Jacob shall be a fire and the house of Joseph a flame and the house of Esau for stubble and they shall kindle in them and devour them and there shall not be any remaining of the house of Esau for the Lord has spoken it. And they of the south shall possess the mount of Esau. And they of the plain, the Philistines, and they shall possess the fields of Ephraim and the fields of Samaria. And Benjamin shall possess Gilead. And the captivity of this host of the children of Israel shall possess that of the Canaanites

> *even unto Zarephath. And the captivity of*
> *Jerusalem which is in Sepharad shall possess*
> *the cities of the south and saviours shall*
> *come up on Mount Zion to judge the mount*
> *of Esau and the kingdom shall be the Lord's."*

The above scripture again reveals that whatever God has designed for you to possess is in the hands of somebody. Now understand that 'possessions' are not necessarily physical items only. They also include your destiny; what you are supposed to become, placement in life and in the Kingdom, favour, blessings, etc. In other words, God is saying He has prepared all these with your name tag on them but 'others' now exercise control over them, spiritually or physically. Whatever comes to you leaves the domain of someone else to you.

However, before all of these will take effect, we need to rediscover our Kingdom identity and reposition ourselves to take back what belongs to us. As we do this, we will begin to see some things change hands. The enemy has held back some valuable things that were originally meant for you. I seek to stir you up to reach out by faith and begin to lay hold on that which God has given you in Christ.

The original arrangement was that God's children shall possess their possessions. Unfortunately, most of their possessions are in the hands of strangers to the Kingdom. As we rediscover our Kingdom identity, God will begin to move on our behalf and divinely shift things in our favour. As you are reading this book, sooner than you think, you are coming to a place of possessing that which God has determined before time began.

There is a parallel in the natural to what we are discussing. There are people whose late parents bequeathed certain properties to them when they were young but some wicked and godless people hijacked what belonged to them. But when they came of age, they stood their ground to reclaim what rightfully belonged to them. They had been theirs all along but the enemies of their destinies illegally possessed them. Unfortunately, this is the scenario with most of us in the Kingdom today. Peradventure you are in such a state, know now that you are no longer a child. Don't sit down helplessly and watch your inheritance elude you.

May the Lord help you to recover your possessions, both naturally and in the Kingdom. It is time for restoration.

> *"Now I say that the heir, as long as he is a child, does not differ at all from a slave, though he is master of all, but is under guardians and stewards until the time appointed by the father" (Gal 4:1-2).*

Beloved, God wants to commit enormous resources into your hands. But as long as you remain 'a child', they will remain in the hands of others till you are matured to take over. So not knowing your position or who you are in the Kingdom will keep you from possessing what has been originally designed for you. However, that is not the intention of God. It is for His people to possess their possessions.

I believe that you are starting a journey to take back that which is yours. There are some things God had planned for you when you were coming into the world, just as He designated for various individuals, families, communities, nations and the Church at large. You have to determine that whatever God has your name on must come to you.

1 Corinthians 3:21 says;
> *"Therefore, let no man glory in men for all things are yours."*

If God says all things are yours, then believe Him and reach out for them. Declare it to yourself that all things are mine and keep saying it to your hearing till your subconscious mind begins to absorb it. If you know that all things are yours, then declare that "healing is mine, blessings are mine, peace is mine, joy is mine, the future is mine, faith is mine, the anointing is mine. Divine wisdom is mine, revelation knowledge and understanding are mine. Divine favor is mine, divine protection, divine health and longevity are mine, the gospel is mine and the Kingdom is mine". If you believe this declaration, pause and pray;

> *"Father, I believe your word that all things are mine, regardless of my experience at this moment, in Jesus' name, Amen".*

Remember, faith comes by constantly hearing the word of God.

"So then faith comes by hearing, and hearing by the word of God" (Rom 10:17).

The unfortunate scenario in the Church today is that most believers have unconsciously placed limitations on themselves because of the pressures life's circumstances have imposed on them. Not only have they limited themselves, they have also limited God in their lives.

> **"Yes, again and again they tempted God, and <u>limited the Holy One of Israel</u>" (Psalm 78:41).**

It is shocking that the all-powerful God with whom nothing is impossible can be limited by man. Our response to the circumstances of life can either limit God or attract His intervention on our behalf.

Another thing that has neutralized the power of the unchangeable word of God in the lives of these believers is their traditional way of thinking.

> **"Making the word of God of no effect through your tradition which you have handed down. And many such things you do" (Mark 7:13).**

It is imperative we realize that the traditions we inherited and the ones we created ourselves can neutralize the power of the infallible word of the living God in our lives. People thus exclude themselves from attaining certain heights in life. Their ability to aspire to higher levels in God has been fatally crushed by these experiences. Sometimes with their own mouth they put a ceiling on their destiny and believe that they cannot achieve certain feats in life. They 'weigh' themselves through their un-renewed mind and say, "no, this is not for me".

If this is your case, I pray that as you read this book, the light of the word of God will enlighten every darkness in your life and propel you to the height God has predestined you for in Christ.

> *"For You will light my lamp; The Lord my God will enlighten my darkness" (Psalm 18:28).*

I counsel you to re-examine in the light of the word of God the traditions you have held so far that have shaped your thinking and make necessary amendments.

> *"For as he thinks in his heart, so is he..." (Proverb 23:7a).*

Your thinking shapes the direction of your life. This is why it is necessary, as believers, to allow the word of God to re-mold our thinking.

> *"Don't become so well-adjusted to your culture that you fit into it without even thinking. Instead, fix your attention on God.*

9

You'll be changed from the inside out. Readily recognize what he wants from you, and quickly respond to it. Unlike the culture around you, always dragging you down to its level of immaturity, God brings the best out of you, develops well-formed maturity in you" (Rom 12:2). THE MESSAGE:

CHAPTER 2
The Purpose Of Possessing Your
POSSESSION

"Then saviors shall come to Mount Zion to judge the mountains of Esau, and the kingdom shall be the Lord's" (Obadiah 21).

It is imperative that we understand the purpose of possessing our possession. Whatever we do not understand the purpose of, we inevitably abuse. In the scripture above, God declared that the reason why He wants His people to possess their possession is for advancing the Kingdom even when we enjoy some. He said *"...it shall be for the Kingdom"*. If we understand the principle of Kingdom priority, it will help us in our relationship with God and people. With that mindset, we can better manage the resources He has committed to our stewardship for His kingdom advancement.

> *"Moreover it is required in stewards that one be found faithful" (Corinthians 4:2).*

The word of God says in Matthew 6:33;

> *"Seek ye first the Kingdom of God and His righteousness and all these other things shall be added unto you".*

So the next thing is that, you must first identify with the Kingdom agenda of God. If you have no Kingdom mindset and agenda, you have nothing to possess in this context because the purpose for possessing is to advance the Kingdom in your daily life.

> *"And you shall remember the Lord your God, for it is He who gives you power to get wealth, that He may establish His covenant which He swore to your fathers, as it is this day" (Deuteronomy 8:18).*

The scriptures reveal that God is the source of whatever we possess. He empowers us to possess wealth in diverse forms. An idea from God can translate into enormous resources at our disposal. For what purpose is all that? Primarily, it is to establish His covenant so that the work of His

Kingdom here on earth will not suffer in our days, but will rather thrive and advance. Therefore, we are only stewards and channels of God's resources. We are to use them in the furtherance of His cause here on earth so that when He requires of us, we will release them.

We see several examples in the scriptures of this principle and practice with God's people. Before Israel left Egypt, the Lord blessed them with wealth from the Egyptians through His favour.

> *"Now the children of Israel had done according to the word of Moses, and they had asked from the Egyptians articles of silver, articles of gold, and clothing. And the Lord had given the people favor in the sight of the Egyptians, so that they granted them what they requested. Thus they plundered the Egyptians" (Exodus 12:35-36).*

As they journeyed in the wilderness, God requested them to bring those resources to build Him a tabernacle.

> *"Then the Lord spoke to Moses, saying: "Speak to the children of Israel, that they bring me an offering. From everyone who gives it willingly with his heart you shall take my offering…*

and let them make me a sanctuary, that I may dwell among them" (Exodus 25:1-8).

But guess what, prior to that the people had influenced Aaron to use them to make an idol, which they all worshipped. Is it not surprising that we sometimes tend to 'idolize' and 'worship' our wealth and resources? We simply forget who gave them to us and withhold them from Him to spend on ourselves. Lord forgive us!

Going further, let's see the classic example of David and his generals. What an example of people who understood the right usage of Kingdom possessions. No wonder they were blessed in their generations and became mighty men.

> *"Moreover, because I have set my affection on the house of my God, I have given to the house of my God, over and above all that I have prepared for the holy house, my own special treasure of gold and silver:.. Then the people rejoiced, for they had offered willingly, because with a loyal heart they had offered willingly to the Lord; and King David also rejoiced greatly" (1 Chronicles 29:3-9).*

In the early New Testament Church, they had the same understanding and attitude. They knew they were stewards of the possessions God gave them and everyone had 'shares' in them. They distributed the blessings corporately. Barnabas took it to the next level. I wonder if it could be replicated in our generation. It is possible, I believe, if we embrace the same principles.

> *"Now the multitude of those who believed were of one heart and one soul; neither did anyone say that any of the things he possessed was his own, but they had all things in common... Nor was there anyone among them who lacked; for all who were possessors of lands or houses sold them, and brought the proceeds of the things that were sold, ...and Joses, who was also named Barnabas by the apostles (which is translated Son of Encouragement), a Levite of the country of Cyprus, having land, sold it, and brought the money and laid it at the apostles' feet"* (Acts 4:32-37).

Even with spiritual gifts, we are to apply the same principles. Jesus gave His disciples power, but quickly made them understand the purpose of it.

> *"And when He had called His twelve disciples to Him, He gave them power over unclean spirits, to cast them out, and to heal all kinds of sickness and all kinds of disease... And as you go, preach, saying, 'the kingdom of heaven is at hand.' 8 Heal the sick, cleanse*

the lepers, raise the dead, cast out demons. Freely you have received, freely give" (Matt 10:1-8).

The anointing we receive is not for our selfish gain. It is for the blessing of others in order to manifest the power of the Kingdom of God. Peter understood that purpose and used it to advance the cause of the Kingdom and set the captives free from bondage.

"Then Peter said, "Silver and gold I do not have, but what I do have I give you: In the name of Jesus Christ of Nazareth, rise up and walk" (Acts 3:6).

May we walk in the same spirit as they did to advance the Kingdom of our Lord God Almighty.

CHAPTER 3
Our True
IDENTITY

"But as many as received Him, to them He gave the right to become children of God, to those who believe in His name" (John 1:12).

Without any shadow of doubt, we have received power to become the sons of God if we have received Jesus Christ as our Lord and personal Saviour. Consequently, we have been blessed with every spiritual blessing in Christ in the heavenly places according to Ephesians 1:3. God predestined us to be received as His children even before the foundation of the world. Before you were born by your parents, God had already earmarked you as a child of God. He knew your name back then. Therefore, if you were known to Him before you came into existence, then settle it in your heart that you are a child of God.

"Just as He chose us in Him before the foundation of the world, that we should be holy and without blame before Him in love, having predestined us to adoption as sons by Jesus Christ to Himself, according to the good pleasure of His will" (Ephesians 1:4).

Romans 8:1 says;

He said *"there is now therefore no condemnation to those who are in Christ Jesus who walk not after the flesh, but after the spirit"*.

Therefore, do not allow the devil or anyone else to condemn and disqualify you as a child of God. If God says you are qualified, nobody has the right to dispute that. Satan twists the scripture to confuse and deceive some Christians. Make no mistake, he can quote scriptures. He quoted Psalm 91 to Jesus that "God will give His angels charge over You". Some Christians don't know where that scripture is. The devil was able to tell Jesus that *"it is written"*. There are things he knows that we are not aware of.

We must come to the place of revelational knowledge to access what God has given to us, lest the enemy takes undue advantage of our ignorance and cheats us. There are provisions of the Kingdom which God has made accessible to us. We have been cheated enough. The time has come to take back what belongs to us. We have been robbed enough and it's time for us to arise and begin to possess our possessions. However, as we have read, until you are fully assured of who you are in the Kingdom, you can do nothing. So if we don't get our reckoning right, we will not have the ability and passion to possess what is ours.

> *"You did not choose Me, but I chose you and appointed you that you should go and bear fruit, and that your fruit should remain, that whatever you ask the Father in My name He may give you" (John 15:16).*

We have been ordained by God to inherit and possess certain resources, both natural and spiritual. He says *"all things are yours."* As you begin to walk in these Kingdom realities, you shall begin to access what you never thought could come your way in your lifetime. God will begin to orchestrate circumstances in your life that will bring you face to face with things and strategic relationships the enemy has hindered you from coming into contact with. You will meet great people who are likeminded.

As you become a Kingdom oriented person, God will bring you into a place of higher capacity of blessing. Remember Jesus said, *"To whom much is given, much is required"*. Abraham was blessed in order for God to bless others through him. God empowers you to become an extension of His blessings to others.

Remember, whatever God will empower you with is already in the hands of others. I see Him shifting and redirecting things to you because you will be a faithful steward of His resources. Be reminded that everything we have was given to us.

> *"For who makes you differ from another? And what do you have that you did not receive? Now if you did indeed receive it, why do you boast as if you had not received it?"* *(1 Corinthians 4:7).*

Beloved, it is imperative that we don't lose sight of this fact.

CHAPTER 4

The Importance Of Kingdom IDENTITY

"The South shall possess the mountains of Esau, and the Lowland shall possess Philistia. They shall possess the fields of Ephraim and the fields of Samaria. Benjamin shall possess Gilead. And the captives of this host of the children of Israel shall possess the land of the Canaanites as far as Zarephath. The captives of Jerusalem who are in Sepharad shall possess the cities of the South. Then saviors shall come to Mount Zion to judge the mountains of Esau, and the kingdom shall be the Lord's" (Obadiah 1:19-21).

What, therefore, is the prerequisite for possessing our possession? It is first knowing our true identity. Let's note here that the Lord mentioned "the house of Jacob". That means we have to come to the place of being able to identify ourselves properly. If we can't identify ourselves as defined by God, we cannot possess anything in His Kingdom. This is what the scripture is talking about. Amazingly in the scripture above, every tribe that God mentioned shall possess some land, that land had some other name on it. God mentioned Philistia and others but He also called out the children of Israel by name and said they shall possess those lands that were already in the possession of others. He was specific. May you also be identified and possess that which is meant for you in Jesus' name.

Beloved, the importance of identity is, if you don't know who you are, you wouldn't know what you qualify for. We therefore have to be serious about possessing and walking in the Kingdom identity else we will not have access to what God has promised us. The main reason is, with the Lord, everything is in the context of the Kingdom of God. Even in the developed world identity is everything. They want to see your identity before they deal with you officially. Oftentimes before you engage in most transactions you will hear them say, "please can

I see your photo ID"? If in this world identity is that important, then it is more important in the spirit. The issue of kingdom identity should therefore not be treated with levity.

Oftentimes, what is given to us is in relation to who we are or what we are perceived to be. For instance, you can walk into a place and simply because of their perception, they accord you a substandard treatment. However, if somebody who knows your true identity steps in and introduces you, their attitude towards you immediately changes. If you had been relegated to a lower place, you are quickly relocated with an apology to where you should be. If you don't know who you are, you will accept what is given to you, even with gratitude. But if you are aware of your true identity as an ambassador of the highest Kingdom, your disposition changes to resonate your 'identity from above', not in pride or arrogance but with humility, knowing it is by grace.

> *"For by grace you have been saved through faith, and that not of yourselves; it is the gift of God, 9 not of works, lest anyone should boast" (Ephesians 2:8-9).*

See the seven sons of Sceva who attempted to cast out an evil spirit from a demon possessed man without the proper credentials and accreditation.

> *"Also there were seven sons of Sceva, a Jewish chief priest, who did so. And the evil spirit answered and said, "Jesus I know, and Paul I know; but who are you?" Then the man in whom the evil spirit was leaped on them, overpowered them, and prevailed against them, so that they fled out of that house naked and wounded" (Acts 19:14-17).*

Strangely, the demon asked for their identity. The possessed man overpowered and beat them mercilessly till they were naked and shamefully driven out from the house. They could not answer the evil spirit appropriately because they were attempting to exercise an authority they didn't have. The Bible described them as 'vagabond Jews' trying to command a demon that was out of control to obey them. Unfortunately for them, the demon knew who they really were. They attempted to function with a counterfeit identity and authority. As a result, they reaped the consequences of their unscrupulous action. It was an ignorance of identity issue they encountered.

Dear friend, your identity matters if you want to advance in the things of God. If you want God to deal with you and the devil to obey your command, then you must be able to show who you are in the Kingdom. Knowing who you are gives you the audacity to take your place in the Kingdom of God and possess your possession.

In every society, there are certain rights and privileges that exclusively belong to certain people. If you are not a citizen you don't have these rights and privileges that are the exclusive reserve of citizens. Citizens can say certain things and get away with them. But if you are not, you better be circumspect and watch how you conduct yourself. For example in USA, you can't just walk into the White House in Washington, DC and demand certain rights if you are holding an Afghanistan passport. But if you are a citizen, you can walk into certain offices and make certain demands because of who you are. Your status as a citizen automatically confers certain privileges on you.

Precious one, in God's Kingdom, identity matters. It determines to a large extent how far you can go in life and how much you can accomplish here on earth. If you don't have that identity, there are certain Kingdom privileges that will elude you. Although they are there for you but because of your 'assumed status' through ignorance, you can't access them. I pray that today you will rediscover your Kingdom identity and begin to lay hold on what God has in store for you.

CHAPTER 5

THE UNIQUENESS

OF YOUR

IDENTITY

"Who once were not a people but are now the people of God, who had not obtained mercy but now have obtained mercy"
(1 Peter 2:10).

We have a pathetic situation today in the Church. Because of an identity crisis in the Church, some of us are trying to look like someone else, rather than discovering our true identity in Christ. Do not desire to look like someone else , but rather be inspired by others to be who God has made you to be. You are uniquely designed by God to accomplish a specific purpose. That is why nobody else among more than seven billion people on planet earth has the same finger print like you. That is amazing!

Unfortunately there are some of us in Church who are aspiring to be like those who are not even in the Kingdom of God. What a pathetic scenario it is that Kingdom citizens desire to be like godless people who have no relationship with God. All their vision in life is to be like someone else in the world. That's absurd. John 3:31 said, *"He that came from above is above all"*. We have all kinds of worldly and ungodly people we have made as role models and want to pattern our lives after. It's unfortunate that many in the Church are not desiring to be like fellow believers who have accomplished great exploits and impacted their world. But if we knew the value of being a Kingdom citizen, we will be striving at any cost to become the people God has designed us to be. Kingdom citizens are priceless and are exalted far above all others.

> *"And raised us up together, and made us sit together in the heavenly places in Christ Jesus". (Ephesians 2:6).*

Sometimes we get confused with worldly things and standards that we abandon our Kingdom pursuits for mere mundane things. Jesus said in John 17:16 that *"Though we are in the world, we are not of the world"*. We are Kingdom people mandated by God to represent Him here on earth. Until we begin to live in that reality and take our place as Kingdom people, certain things reserved by God to express Kingdom wisdom, power and wealth will elude us. I see many reading this book becoming functional ambassadors of the Kingdom.

The whole fight of the devil against humanity in general and believers in particular is about their God given identity. Every effort of Satan is to put your identity in question. God said in Genesis 1:26, *"Let us make man in our own image according to our likeness"*. He knows the certainty of the command to make man in God's image. So he does everything possible to distort it in our minds since he could not stop it neither can he really alter it. At the end of creation, God was pleased with everything He had made and declared that it was very good.

"Then God saw everything that He had made, and indeed it was very good. So the evening and the morning were the sixth day" (Genesis 1:3).

Certainly, creation was exactly what God intended. There was no ambiguity at all.

In Genesis chapter 3, the devil came to the woman and said; *"has God said you should not eat of every tree in the garden? ...the Lord knows that the day you eat of it you shall be like Him". (Gen 3:1-5).* His primary interest was to confuse her identity. But the Bible said; *"In the likeness of God he made them, male and female".* There was no question about their identity. They were already in the likeness and image of God. So how come the devil now tells the woman *"the day you will eat of this fruit you will become like God".* The woman forgot she was already like God and believed the lie of the devil. She proceeded and took the fruit, ate it and gave some to her husband. From that day, their identity changed. How sad! When God came in the cool of the day to fellowship with them as usual, they ran for cover because of their nakedness. God said to the man; *"Adam where are you"? And he said, "I heard your voice in the garden and I hid myself because I was naked".* And God said; *"Who told you are naked"?*

Distorted Identity

> *"Then the eyes of both of them were opened, and they knew that they were naked; and they sewed fig leaves together and made themselves coverings" (Genesis 3:7).*

After Adam and Eve ate the fruit, they lost their true identity and realized they were naked and became ashamed. The devil probably made a mockery of them, (as is typical of him) saying "now you are naked, you thought you had become like God". When they were like God, His glory covered them but as soon as they allied with Satan and disobeyed God, they lost the glory that hitherto had covered their nakedness. Consequently, their identity immediately was distorted. That is Satan's objective till date. They became ashamed of themselves and started hiding and covering their nakedness from each other. But prior to that, they had been walking around the garden naked and unashamed.

When you are in your house alone or with your spouse, you can freely walk around naked without any restraint. But as soon as you hear the voice of a stranger you run for cover. (There are things that outsiders don't have the right to see). After they lost their true identity, God became 'a stranger' to them. From that time forward, because their identity changed, they began running away from God who was their 'clothing' and their covering hitherto.

It is comfortable walking with someone who is at the same level as you are, but as soon as the levels change it becomes a struggle to maintain that relationship. That was the problem that set in after the fall of man. But thank God the Lord Jesus came and restored us back to the exalted position as sons of God.

> *"And raised us up together, and made us sit together in the heavenly places in Christ Jesus" (Ephesians 2:6).*

Because a lot of us don't understand the dynamics of our relationship with Jesus Christ, we are "running around like naked people", seeking for 'covering' where there is indeed no real cover. Wherever you are taking a false refuge today, may the Lord bring you out and give you real covering to live a triumphant life as a Kingdom citizen.

The devil went after the identity of Adam and Eve and got it. Everybody in the scriptures Satan dealt with was all about their identity. He did it all the way to the Lord Jesus Christ, but woefully failed because Jesus knew without doubt who He was and stood His ground through the Word. So will he come after yours but don't lose sight of who you are in Christ.

> *"And the devil said to Him, "If You are the Son of God, command this stone to become bread." But Jesus answered him, saying, "It is written, 'Man shall not live by bread alone, but by every word of God" (Luke 4:3-4).*

When Christ came on the scene, the Father declared, *"This is my beloved son in whom I am well pleased"*. Everybody present heard it. Satan also heard it. When Jesus went into the wilderness to fast and pray, after forty days Satan came and said to him according to the scriptures;

> *"If you are the son of God, turn these stones into bread" and also "jump down from this tower and the angels of God will protect you".*

In other words, Satan comes to test your conviction of who you are. He will even lure you with scriptures to do things contrary to the will of God in order to prove your Kingdom identity. You must not let down your guard, or else he could take undue advantage of such vulnerable moments. The Father had already declared who Jesus was so He didn't need the devil's validation.

There are times you have to tell the devil, *"I know who I am in Christ"* because only God the Father authenticates and qualifies you as a child of God.

Beloved, if you are a child of God, washed in the precious blood of Jesus, then you have power to do whatever God has ordained. Tell the devil that your name is indelibly written in Heaven.

> **"Nevertheless do not rejoice in this, that the spirits are subject to you, but rather rejoice because your names are written in heaven"(Luke10:20).**

Furthermore, 1 John 4:17, says that;
> **"... As He is, so are we in this world"**
> **(1 John 4:17).**

CHAPTER 6

Our Reserved
INHERITANCE

"As His divine power has given to us all things that pertain to life and godliness, through the knowledge of Him who called us by glory and virtue" (2 Peter 1:3-4).

Anything that has your name tag on it, has been uniquely designed and reserved exclusively for you. That is what the Word of God says He has done for us in His Kingdom. We have an inheritance reserved for us to possess. One day we shall all stand before Jesus Christ to give an account of how we lived our lives on earth. Some of us will be shocked as to how much was designed for us that we never experienced while on earth. We will realize we had so much at our disposal that we never touched. May God help us now to see and access them. I pray that for the rest of your life here on earth, you will experience all that God has in store for you to expand His Kingdom for His glory. You will possess what He wants you to have in Jesus' name. Amen.

Beloved, there is more to just attending church. There are things God wants us to inherit in our lifetime than sitting in church day in and day out. Your destiny has been tailored according to what is written in the volume of the books of God.

> *"Then I said, "Behold, I come; in the scroll of the book it is written of me" (Psalm 40:7).*

More anointed preachers are still going to manifest in times to come. More wealthy people are coming on the scene. More great scientists and scholars are going to be showcased. More anointed singers and musicians are going to be seen. More anointed authors of books are to be released. More excellent politicians, technocrats, business men and women are going to show up. All because there is coming an unusual outpouring of the Spirit of God on the earth in these last days. We will witness a generation of believers that will be an express revelation of the fullness of God in every aspect of life in their generation. There is a rising generation. The

scripture had said that the glory of the latter house
shall be more than the glory of the former. This
latter church is not made by human hands like
in the old, it is not a building, they are human
lives built and fashioned by God to express His
fullness and save as many as possible from the
corruption of the ephemeral world.

We have been given unfettered access to the
throne of grace to bring down some things that
will improve people's lives and advance God's
Kingdom. Please hear my counsel, quit sitting
in church doing nothing. You may be one of the
prophetic voices God is raising in these last days.
Move out of your comfort zone and take hold of
God in your closet so that you can begin to access
the grace waiting for you to act in faith. God said;

"Open your mouth wide and I will fill it"
(Psalm 81:10).

You may have an anointed voice of a psalmist
to lead your generation into the presence of
God through inspired songs and bring God's
presence down on earth. Don't lock up that
voice in your bathroom and kitchen. Heaven
and earth want to hear your voice and give glory
to God. Join the choir in your church or your

school, with one thing in mind; to express the Kingdom life in you. Creation is waiting for your manifestation.

> *"For the earnest expectation of the creation eagerly waits for the revealing of the sons of God" (Romans 8:19).*

Become a vessel prepared for the Master's use that when you speak or sing, the sick are healed, sinners are convicted and reconciled with God, the hopeless see hope rising again for them, the broken hearted are healed, the oppressed are delivered, captives are set free, the confused get direction in life, relationships are mended and finally our God is glorified. Stop sitting on the grace in you. Paul said stir up your gift.

> *"Therefore I remind you to stir up the gift of God which is in you through the laying on of my hands" (2 Timothy1:6).*

If you do not step out in faith, you cannot possess your possession. When I talk about possessing your possession, again please don't only think about material things but of the spiritual as well. If you possess your God given possessions spiritually, they will ultimately deliver whatever material things you need to advance God's kingdom and live a better life here on earth. What I am saying in essence is that do not put the cart before the horse. Have your priorities right.

> **"Seek first the kingdom of God and His righteousness, and all these things shall be added to you" (Matthew 6:33).**

Set your mind on things above like an anointing that will come upon your life to do great exploits for the Kingdom, the power of God that you will access to help people who are struggling under all kinds of demonic shackles. Think of great grace that will come upon your life to do the uncommon. There are people that have many degrees and still have amounted to nothing in life. Their lives are miserable to the core. Jesus said in Luke 12:15 that, *"our lives are not measured by abundance of the things we have acquired"*. Many therefore have not found their Kingdom assignment. It is not a surprise they are still unfulfilled despite all they have.

> **"If then you were raised with Christ, seek those things which are above, where Christ is, sitting at the right hand of God. Set your mind on things above, not on things on the earth" (Colossians 3:1-2).**

39

Man was not designed to find fulfillment in material things but in discovering and working out God's purpose for his life. This scenario explains why some wealthy people commit suicide in spite of all they have. There are people who have all the properties they will ever need in life and still have no joy. They have all kinds of human relationships but lack the joy that comes from within. Their hearts are still yearning for something more, something they can't even explain. This is the mystery of their agony; they have not come into contact with the reason why they exist. These folks have not come in touch with their Kingdom mandate. Until they realize what makes them who they are, they may never find contentment in life. The reason why their internal and external struggles never seem to end is because they have not possessed Kingdom possessions.

The day you realize who you are, your journey to possessing your possessions begins. Deep inside your spirit, you will be persuaded about your true identity. Though sometimes the outside may attempt to contradict what's inside, don't buckle. If you step into your possession, your spirit will be at ease and you will know you are there. At that point, let the earth quake, seas roar, the forces of life be arrayed against you, hordes of demons rise up against you, you will not be shaken but rather be at peace. You will know that you are doing what God wants you to do and you are where God wants you to be.

If you are sitting in church confused and frustrated, the reason could be that you have not entered into the possession God has marked for you. I pray that you will be divinely provoked as you learn these things and lay hold of the purpose for which God called and saved you. If you are still wandering not knowing what life holds for you, I pray that you will come to the place where you will understand and become who God says you are.

Our Reserved Inheritance

CHAPTER 7

Renewing Your Kingdom IDENTITY

"And be renewed in the spirit of your mind, and that you put on the new man which was created according to God, in true righteousness and holiness" *(Ephesians 4:23-24).*

God is specific about what He wants you to possess. There are certain things (both spiritual and physical) you are qualified for as a child of God who represents the Kingdom. They are mandated to come to you. If you lack this understanding, you can make all the noise about possessing your possession and still end up possess nothing. Therefore, in order for you to have access to those specific things, you have to straighten up your Kingdom identity, peradventure it is expired.

In real life experience, when your identity card expires, what do you do? You renew it by fulfilling all obligations required for renewal. I am persuaded that this is the season of renewing Kingdom identity. Your Kingdom identity may have 'expired' several years ago. No matter how long you have walked with an 'expired identity,' it is crucial to the moment. What is urgently required now is to summon up courage and "pay the price" for renewal. The 'currency' is your faith as a child of God. As you step out in faith to rediscover your identity in the word of God, I see your Kingdom identity being renewed! The good news is that the latter is brighter than the former.

> *"Arise, shine; for your light has come! And the glory of the Lord is risen upon you"* *(Isaiah 60:1).*

What will make you stand out there in the world plagued by confusion, hopelessness and misery is your Kingdom identity;

> *"Now when these things begin to happen, look up and lift up your heads, because your redemption draws near" (Luke 21:28).*

Your identity matters greatly, therefore guard it jealously. As the coming of our Lord Jesus Christ draws near, beloved, nothing matters more than making sure that your Kingdom identity is current and valid. The coming of the Lord is very near and He is coming for His Kingdom citizens, not church members! You can be in church and be alienated from the life of God. The fact that one is in church does not make him a Kingdom citizen. You could be in a country and still be illegally resident. Remember, when Israel left Egypt, the Bible says a mixed multitude left with them. That did not change their identity as Egyptians or strangers.

If you have been in church but you know in your heart that you are not a Kingdom citizen (that is you are not genuinely saved), pause for a moment and pray this simple but powerful prayer with me immediately:

> *"Father in the name of Jesus, I acknowledge that though I have been in church, I am cut off from the life of God. Therefore, I repent from my sins. Now oh Lord, I make a decision that will change my life forever. I believe that Jesus Christ is the Son of God and He died for my sins and He was raised from the dead the third day for my salvation. I confess Him as*

Lord of all and my personal Lord and Savior. Thank you Father for granting me eternal life in Jesus' name. Amen".

God bless you for praying.

Yes, I said Kingdom citizens are those the Lord is coming for, not church members. Because Jesus said; *"on that day (when I come) many shall come to me and say Lord, Lord, we did all these things in your name and I will say to them, I never knew you". (Matthew 7:22-23).* The difference is that you were in the church, but your identity probably was long expired (backslidden) or you never had a Kingdom identity because you have never been a citizen of the Kingdom (not really received Jesus as your Lord and Saviour). You were just "playing church", not living the Kingdom life. You were not identified as a Kingdom minded person; you were not involved with the things of the Kingdom of God. Now therefore, resolve to move from playing around church to becoming a Kingdom addicted person.

> *"But seek first the kingdom of God and His righteousness, and all these things shall be added to you" (Matthew 6:33).*

That is how we can begin to possess our unique possessions. If we don't get our identity issue corrected or updated, we cannot have access to the things that have been freely given to us by God, because it is only by the Spirit of God we can access them before their physical manifestation.

"Now we have received, not the spirit of the world, but the Spirit who is from God, that we might know the things that have been freely given to us by God" (1 Corinthians 2:12).

Resolve to take back your identity in Christ. If we are able to get it straightened up, certain things will begin to fall into place naturally. You may not need to struggle for them. They will just come to you. There is much reserved for you and therefore make sure you reconnect to your Kingdom identity.

"O Lord, You are the portion of my inheritance and my cup; you maintain my lot. The lines have fallen to me in pleasant places; Yes, I have a good inheritance" (Psalm 16:5-6).

My desire and prayer for everyone reading this book is to become a Kingdom addicted person and by the eyes of faith I can see that happening.

I can see God steering the hearts of people who will dare to believe Him for a radical change in their lives. Jesus Christ will be coming for a glorious, spotless Church devoid of any form of wrinkles and blemishes.

> *"That He might present her to Himself a glorious church, not having spot or wrinkle or any such thing, but that she should be holy and without blemish" (Ephesians 5:27).*

Sometimes we doubt our true identity in Christ due to the effects of some negative circumstances we have experienced in life. The damaging effect of that is, as we allow those experiences to leave imprints on our minds, over time they begin to redefine our identity. Some of us take it to the extreme where we begin to gradually lose our confidence to stand before God, to deal with the battles of life and make demands for our Kingdom rights and privileges.

No matter where you are on the stage of life, I want to reassure you in your spirit and in your mind that if you are still a child of God, you belong to the Kingdom that cannot be shaken, even when everything else in our world is being shaken.

"Therefore, since we are receiving a kingdom which cannot be shaken, let us have grace, by which we may serve God acceptably with reverence and godly fear" (Hebrews 12:28).

God has promised that you will possess your possessions and therefore it shall come to pass. Not because you have cried enough to earn it, but because you have the Kingdom right to claim them. I see it happening for you. I see it coming to you in the name of Jesus.

CHAPTER 8
Refuse To Be
DISPOSSESSED

"Watch, stand fast in the faith, be brave, be strong" (1 Corinthians 16:13).

Sometimes we find ourselves in circumstances that tend to dispossess us of what the Lord has given to us. Again, these refer to both spiritual and physical things. Some of those circumstances might be the consequences of our actions or inactions. Others could be events in our lives we had no hand in. There are people who were born into hopeless situations until the grace of God intervened and altered the course of their lives. But thanks be to God who rescues us from such precarious situations.

"Shall the prey be taken from the mighty, or the captives of the righteous be delivered? But thus says the Lord: "Even the captives of

> *the mighty shall be taken away, and the prey*
> *of the terrible be delivered; for I will contend*
> *with him who contends with you, and I will*
> *save your children" (Isa 49:24-25).*

There was a man in scripture called Mephibosheth who was a grandson of Saul. When David became king, he asked;

> *"Is there anybody left in the house of Saul*
> *that I can show kindness to"? And then one*
> *called Ziba came out and said, "Oh, there is*
> *one, Mephibosheth, the son of Jonathan; he's*
> *in the land called Lodebar and he is lame".*
> *2 Samuel 9:1-5).*

Lodebar means a place of forgetfulness. Why and how did he end up in Lodebar? A maidservant in a bid to save him while running for safety, accidentally dropped him on the ground. As a result his legs were fractured and he became lame. If the maid had not dropped him, he wouldn't have been lame in the first place because he was born whole and complete. Indeed there are some who due to no fault of theirs have ended up in disadvantaged situations.

When King David heard of it, he commanded that the young boy be brought to his palace and

Mephibosheth ended up dinning with him on the same table. The king said, to him: "You don't belong to Lodebar. From today, you will sit at my table because this is where you belong. You are royalty. I made a covenant with your father Jonathan, that I will show kindness to him and his seed after him. You will therefore sit at my table the rest of your life". "So David said to him;

> *"Do not fear, for I will surely show you kindness for Jonathan your father's sake, and will restore to you all the land of Saul your grandfather; and you shall eat bread at my table continually. Then he bowed himself, and said, "What is your servant, that you should look upon such a dead dog as I?" (2 Samuel 9:7-8).*

Because of the effects of the negative circumstances of his life, Mephibosheth had concluded that he was good for nothing. He referred to himself as "a dead dog" not even a living one. Never allow the circumstances of your life to redefine your identity. Rather, let your Kingdom identity define your circumstances. Imagine the damaging impact Mephibosheth's interpretation of his situation had on his mind. His personality had been severely crushed by his life's experience. If you allow the devil, he will take undue advantage of your life's challenges and reduce you to a crust of bread.

Mephibosheth was promoted to the king's table, but still saw himself unworthy of royalty. You can 'sit at the King's table' (be a child of God) and yet see yourself as unworthy. That mindset has to change. I see your old mindset being taken away from you right now and a new one being given you as you assimilate the message in this book.

May the Lord give you the ability to understand your position of royalty in Jesus' name. Amen.

> *"But you are a special people, a holy nation, priests and kings, a people given up completely to God, so that you may make clear the virtues of him who took you out of the dark into the light of heaven"* (1 Peter 2:9). BBE

This is the situation with some believers today in the Kingdom. They have been brought to the place of stepping out in faith to possess their possession but they are 'incarcerated' in their past experiences. They are making no attempt to move into the position God has set before them.

May you rediscover your Kingdom identity in Christ, so you don't remain a victim of the past and your old distorted identity.

"And you have made them a kingdom (royal race) and priests to our God, and they shall reign [as kings] over the earth!" (Rev 5:10). AMP

Don't be like Peter who experienced angelic deliverance from prison. While he was stepping out of prison, the doors were opening by themselves. Yet after he came out, he thought he was still in prison until the angel roused him and said "Peter, you are out of the prison. Start moving forward or else you will lose your deliverance"! It was possible for the soldiers to have put him back in jail. The Bible says he thought he was dreaming.

"So the angel went out and Peter followed. He did not know if the angel was really doing this. He thought he might be seeing a vision" (Acts 12:9). Easy-to-Read Version

There are certain deliverances God has wrought in some people's lives that they are still struggling to come to terms with. Yes, they are real.

"When the Lord brought back the captivity of Zion, We were like those who dream" (Psalm 126:1).

But when we fail to move away from the circumstances God has delivered us from, the enemy will return and attempt to lure us back into that same prison environment. That is why we are instructed to renew our minds in Romans 12:2, so we can start thinking like God and see what He has accomplished for us in Christ. The battle ground is our mind and we must rise up to the challenge.

> *"Don't change yourselves to be like the people of this world, but let God change you inside with a new way of thinking. Then you will be able to decide and accept what God wants for you. You will be able to know what is good and pleasing to him and what is perfect"* *(Romans 12:2). Bible: Easy-to-Read Version*

We have been set free by the power of the Lord Jesus Christ, but some believers have been 'rearrested and sent back to the jail' of sickness, failure, poverty, fear, offense, hopelessness and doubt. There is something better for you in Christ than what you have ever seen. You must come to a place where you resolve to tell the enemy, "enough is enough"! If you change your position, some things will change in your life.

Galatians 5:1 says;
"Stand therefore in the liberty wherewith Christ has set you free. And be not entangled again with the yoke of bondage".

There were four lepers who were sitting by the gate of Samaria, ostracized. They said, *"Why should we sit here till we die?* Let us make a move. We cannot do much, but we'll try and do something. Let us go to the camp of the Assyrians, if they kill us, we are ready to die. If they save us, fine. But let us, at least, make an effort". Those lepers did not know that God had already released a prophetic word of blessing. When they stepped into the word, they were able to possess enough and said "we are not doing right, we have to send the good news to the people who are locked up in 'the prison' of Samaria". Those lepers stepped into a prophecy that changed them. They became rich overnight. Despite your situation, you can walk into the promises of God that will affect your destiny. Let that happen today.

For some people, until they walk into the promises of God, they will make it difficult for those who will read their tributes. But it should not be so for you. By the time you finish your course here on earth, may people rejoice over you. May they say you made an impact. May they say you changed some lives. May they say you saved some souls. May they say by your anointing they were healed. May they say that God used you to glorify Himself in their lives. I prophesy that upon your life. At the end of your life, may people celebrate you. May you possess your Kingdom identity and become who God says you are as you walk in your new identity.

Walking In Your New Identity

> *"Therefore, if anyone is in Christ, he is a new creation; old things have passed away; behold, all things have become new" (2 Corinthians 5:17).*

We have to mentally come out of the various prison houses we have locked ourselves in. In fact when we step into Christ, we are no more there. We receive a new identity because the blood of Jesus is enough to wash, cleanse and sanctify us.

> *"Our soul has escaped as a bird from the snare of the fowlers; the snare is broken, and we have escaped" (Psalm 124: 7).*

In Him, you can be who you never thought you could ever be. The truth is we are sitting around so much in the Kingdom while playing around as if we have nothing. That is not the will of God. We have it all at our disposal, so be bold and courageous to walk in your new identity. In real life people come out of prison and become great and successful. They put the past behind them and strive to establish a new identity and reputation. So can we in Christ.

You have to realize that the devil is busy trying to change our identity. He wants to attack us with sickness and call us sick people, but in the books of God we have been healed. He's trying hard to bring us back into sin and bondage, back to old friends and the former ways of life. But we must resist him by prayer and steadfastness in Christ and the word of God. That is why it is important to be in a Word based church and to be in good fellowship so that we stay strong and prevail. May the Lord help us.

Finally, precious one, you may be saying now that, "these things concern me and I am interested, but I don't know how to access them". Well, if you have not received Jesus as your personal Lord and Saviour, you need Him in your life now to do so. Therefore, please pray this prayer aloud, believing with all your heart.

PRAYER OF SALVATION

Father in Heaven, I believe Jesus Christ is the Son of God. He died and rose again for my sins. Please forgive me all my sins. Lord, please come into my heart, be my Lord and personal Saviour and make me a child of God. In Jesus' name I pray, Amen.

God bless you and keep you. May you possess all that God has ordained for you in Christ Jesus.

OTHER BOOKS AUTHORED BY JESSE SACKEY

I believe that reading this book *"Possessing the Kingdom"* has reawakened your consciousness of who you are in Christ and what God has made available for you in the Kingdom. In that same depth and revelation, the author has succinctly written the under listed books and manuals with clarity of purpose. Therefore, we invite you to take the advantage of getting copies for yourself and your loved ones.

- *The Lost Church*
- *The Kingdom Series*
- *Times and Seasons of God*
- *The Importance of the Prophetic*
- *Concept and Practices in Ministry*
- *Things That Accompany Salvation*
- *The "Becoming" Series among others*

For inquiries on how to get copies of the under listed books and manuals, contact the author via email at *revjesses1@gmail.com*